MYTHICAL CREATURES

Vampires

Charlotte Guillain

Raintree

Chicago, Illinois

www.heinemannraintree.com
Visit our website to find out
more information about
Heinemann-Raintree books.

To order:
☎ Phone 888-454-2279
💻 Visit www.heinemannraintree.com
to browse our catalog and order online.

Edited by Adrian Vigliano, Rebecca Rissman,
and Nancy Dickmann
Designed by Joanna Hinton Malivoire
Levelling by Jeanne Clidas
Original illustrations by Christian Slade
Picture research by Elizabeth Alexander
Production by Victoria Fitzgerald
Printed and bound in China by CTPS

14 13 12 11 10
10 9 8 7 6 5 4 3 2 1

**Library of Congress Cataloging-in-
Publication Data**
Guillain, Charlotte.
  Vampires / Charlotte Guillain.
    p. cm.—(Mythical creatures)
  Includes bibliographical references and index.
  ISBN 978-1-4109-3801-5 (hc)—ISBN 978-1-4109-
3808-4 (pb) 1. Vampires—Juvenile literature. I.
Title.
  GR830.V3G85 2011
  398.21—dc22   2009052414

Acknowledgments
The author and publishers are grateful to the
following for permission to reproduce copyright
material: Alamy pp. **8** (© Pictorial Press Ltd), **14**
(© Jack Carey), **16** (© Ariadne Van Zandbergen),
17 (© Steven Poe), **23** (© imagebroker), **25**
(© imagebroker); © Austen Zaleski p. **11**; Corbis
pp. **10** (© Michael & Patricia Fogden), **22**
(© Mike Grandmaison); Getty Images pp. **9**
(Scott Mansfield/Photographer's Choice), **21**
(Karen Moskowitz/Stone+), **24** (Hulton Archive);
iStockphoto p. **13** bottom (© oana vinatoru);
Photolibrary pp. **19** (Caroline Penn/Imagestate),
28 (Nick Gordon/OSF); © Stephanie Hu p. **20**;
The Kobal Collection p. **29** (Maverick Films).

Every effort has been made to contact copyright
holders of any material reproduced in this book.
Any omissions will be rectified in subsequent
printings if notice is given to the publisher.

Some words are shown in bold, **like this.** You can find
out what they mean by looking in the glossary.

Contents

What Is a Mythical Creature?

A **myth** is a story people tell over many years. Many of these stories are about **mythical** creatures. But are the creatures real? People tell stories of unicorns. Do you think they are real?

Have you ever heard stories about werewolves? Do you think they really exist?

What Is a Vampire?

People around the world have been scared of vampires for hundreds of years. Many of these creatures look like humans. Stories say vampires come out at night and suck human blood.

DID YOU KNOW?

Count Dracula is one of the most famous vampires. The book *Dracula* was written over 100 years ago.

Many stories tell of vampires who lie in coffins or graveyards in the daytime. They hunt for **victims** at night. They bite people with **fangs** and suck their blood.

DID YOU KNOW?
Some stories say vampires don't have a reflection or a shadow.

9

The Vampire Myth

People all over the world tell stories about vampires. The **myths** may have started with real blood-sucking animals, such as vampire bats.

vampire bat

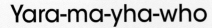

Yara-ma-yha-who

DID YOU KNOW?

Australian **aboriginal** people have myths about Yara-ma-yha-who (say *yarra-ma-ya-hoo*). It is a small vampire that sucks blood from **victims** using suckers on its fingers.

Vampires of Europe

There are many vampire **myths** in Eastern Europe. In Serbia a vampire called Sava Savanovic (say *sa-va sa-va-no-vitch*) was supposed to live in a **watermill**. Stories say he killed people who came to the mill and drank their blood.

Europe

Serbia

Romania

Greece

Sava Savanovic

Myths say Dracula lived in this castle.

DID YOU KNOW?

Many people think that Transylvania, Romania, is the home of vampires. This myth was started in the book *Dracula*.

wooden stake

holy water

HOLY † WATER

crucifix

Myths from Europe say that a hawthorn branch or garlic keeps vampires away. A **crucifix** or holy water could also work. Myths say that putting a wooden **stake** through a vampire's heart kills it.

Lamia

DID YOU KNOW?

Ancient Greek myths tell about a blood-sucking creature called Lamia (say *la-mee-ah*). She sucked children's blood at night.

Vampires of Africa

There are many vampire **myths** in West Africa. The Adze (say *ad-zay*) was a vampire who turned into a firefly. It went into homes at night and sucked the blood of **victims**.

DID YOU KNOW?

The Owenga (say *oh-wen-gah*) was a West African vampire that sucked blood from the thumb of sleeping humans.

This Makonde (say *mack-on-day*) vampire mask comes from Tanzania.

Africa

Tanzania

The Asanbosam (say *ah-san-bo-sam*) lived in West African forests. It had iron teeth and hooks on its feet. It used its hooks and claws to scoop **victims** up into the trees.

bells

DID YOU KNOW?
Some people in Africa kept vampires away by:
- ringing small bells
- carving a post in their house

Vampires of Asia

Vampire **myths** are also told in Asia. In China the Jiang Shi (say *jee-ang shee*) was a dead body that killed people to get life from them. It had **moldy** skin and long white hair.

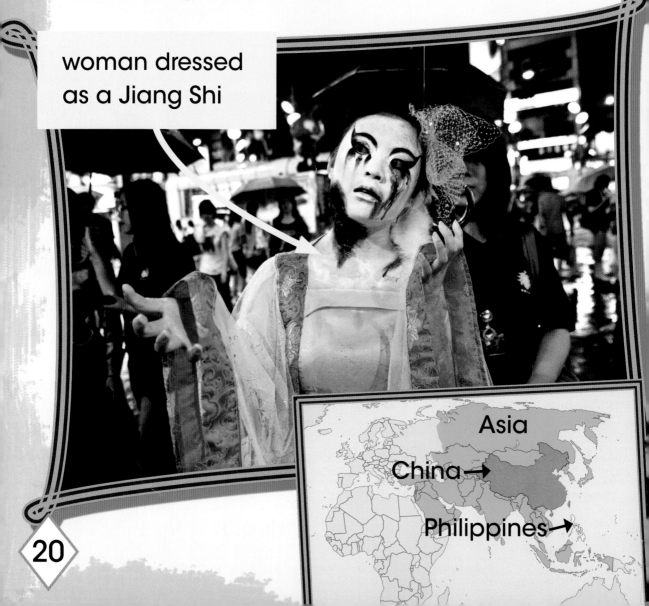

woman dressed as a Jiang Shi

Asia

China →

Philippines →

In the Philippines the Mandurugo (say *man-doo-roo-go*) was a girl during the day. At night she grew wings and a long tongue to suck blood from sleeping **victims**.

Vampires of North and South America

In Colombia the Tunda (say *toon-dah*) was a female vampire who could **shape-shift**. She turned into a beautiful woman. Then she took men to the forest and sucked their blood.

North America

Mexico

Colombia

South America

The Nahuatl Indians in Mexico believed in vampires called Tlaciques (say *tuh-la-see-kways*). These vampires were witches who turned into balls of flame.

23

Close Relatives

Other **mythical** creatures around the world are similar to vampires. The zombie is another **undead** creature. It is a dead body that has been brought back to life.

zombies

lightning bird

DID YOU KNOW?

Myths say the African lightning bird **shape-shifts** to look like a man and then sucks **victims'** blood.

Could Vampires Exist?

What do you think?

 They could be real...

- People all over the world tell stories about vampires.

 I'm not so sure...

- Stories can be made up. Many stories all over the world are similar.

 They could be real...

- Vampires live in coffins and dark places so we may not be able to see them.

 I'm not so sure...

- Vampire stories are just made up to scare people.

 **They could be real...**

- Something has really bitten people in their sleep and sucked their blood.

 I'm not so sure...

- People could have been bitten by a vampire bat or a biting insect.

The truth is that vampires don't really exist. But they make a great story!

Reality Versus Myth

Vampire bat (real)

Found: Central and South America

Lives: Caves, trees, old buildings

Eats: Blood of birds and animals, sometimes humans

Special power: Uses **echolocation** to find its way in the dark

Seen: With an **infrared** camera

Vampire (myth)

Found: All over the world

Lives: Coffins, graveyards, forests

Eats: Human blood

Special power: Hard to kill

Seen: In movies and books

Glossary

aboriginal first people living in Australia

crucifix model of a Christian cross

echolocation using the sound of echoes to find the way

fangs long, sharp teeth

infrared special kind of light used to show things in the dark

moldy covered in a layer of fungus

myth traditional story, often about magical creatures and events

mythical found in myths

shape-shift change the way someone or something looks

stake pointed stick

undead something that has died but is somehow still moving among the living

victim person who is attacked

watermill building with machinery to grind flour using power from moving water

Find Out More

Books

Besel, Jennifer M. *Vampires*. Mankato, MN: Capstone Press, 2007.

Knox, Barabara. *Castle Dracula: Romania's Vampire Home.* New York, NY: Bearport Publishing, 2005.

Somervill, Barbara A. *Vampire Bats: Hunting for Blood*. New York, NY: Powerkids Press, 2007.

Websites

http://animals.nationalgeographic.com/ animals/mammals/common-vampire-bat.html
Learn all about the vampire bat at this National Geographic Website.

www.fieldmuseum.org/mythiccreatures/index. html
Learn about more mythical creatures at the Field Museum's Mythic Creatures Exhibit Website.

Index